CONGRATULATIONS

365 DAYS OF DECLARATIONS FOR EVERYDAY LIFE

Joe Louis Ingram, Jr.

ISBN 978-1-68601-958-6

Unless otherwise noted, all scripture quotations are from the King James Version (KJV) of the *Holy Bible*.

INTRODUCTION

CONGRATULATIONS is declaring the word that God has already spoken over your life, and to begin the process of healing from any situation that has negatively impacted your life. A lack of money, family challenges, or career problems are all things that can offset us, but we must begin the practice of congratulating ourselves based on the promises God has given us rather than complaining about our circumstances. Romans 4:17 encourages us to "speak those things that be not as though they were."

Jeremiah 29:11 states, "For I know the plans I have for you, declares the Lord, plans for welfare and not for evil, to give you a future and a hope" (ESV).

Congratulate when others hate, when you want to procrastinate, and when you feel like you are late in life. Talk yourself into blessing: you are a direct summation of what you speak. Most of the time I believe we are caught off guard, or we have not properly healed from past experiences, but that once we begin to declare a thing, that is when the deliverance will take place.

Congratulations! You are about to enter a new season of speaking a new language of faith and hope over your family, friends, jobs, churches, and most importantly, your life. Instead of thinking and speaking destructively; begin to think positively toward your destiny. Pat yourself on the back and congratulate yourself with God's word. When Christ congratulates you, you have a reason to congratulate yourself.

His word declares:

> *For my thoughts are not your thoughts, neither are your ways my ways, declares the LORD. For as the heavens are higher than the earth, so are my ways higher than your ways and my thoughts than your thoughts.* (Isaiah 55:8–9)

**In loving memory of
Pastor Joe L. Ingram, Sr.
March 23, 1936 - Jan 31, 2012**

"I see no defeat for God is on my side."

FORWARD

To anyone who is looking to experience better in life, it is important that you understand that you are the creator of your own experience! Because of this fact, you must understand that what you focus on the most is what will expand in your life and in this book, *Congratulations*, Joe Ingram gives us a model and a guide as well as the verbal "know how" in speaking your better life now. This book is becoming a favorite among those who are serious about succeeding in next level living.

I have been blessed with the joy and the excitement of the daily opportunity to speak life into my circumstance and future. Thank you, Joe Ingram, for being used by God to bring understanding and opportunity through this powerful literary work, *Congratulations*. This is a must-read and is easy to follow for all.

To your success, Congratulations!
Dr. Adrian Blue, Sr.
Better Life Coach and Spiritual Teacher
Better Life "the Movement" Church
Betterlifeseeker.com

DAY 1

Congratulations!

Happy New Year and New You!

Therefore, if any man be in Christ, he is a new creature: old things are passed away; behold, all things are become new.

-- 2 Corinthians 5:17

Congratulations!

You are the result of when a God thing happens...

So God created man in His *own* image, in the image of God created He him; male and female created He them.

-- Genesis 1:27

Congratulations!

(State your name), you are in line for a miracle!

He performs wonders that cannot be fathomed, miracles that cannot be counted.

-- Job 5:9, NIV

DAY 4

Congratulations!

Give yourself a standing ovation every day! Your help comes from the Lord.

I will lift up mine eyes unto the hills, from whence cometh my help. My help cometh from the LORD, which made heaven and earth.

-- Psalm 121:1-2

Congratulations!

The favor of God has overtaken you.

For the LORD God is a sun and shield:
the LORD will give grace and glory: no
good thing will he withhold from them that
walk uprightly.

-- Psalm 84:11

Congratulations!

Your season has shifted into acceleration mode.

But by shifting our focus from what we do to what God does, don't we cancel out all our careful keeping of the rules and ways God commanded? Not at all. What happens, in fact, is that by putting that entire way of life in its proper place, we confirm it.

-- Romans 3:31, MSG

12

DAY 7

Congratulations!

You have taken off into another dimension.

May be able to comprehend with all saints what is the breadth, and length, and depth, and height;

-- Ephesians 3:18

Congratulations!

You are anointed, appointed, and called by God.

But the anointing which ye have received of Him abides in you, and ye need not that any man teach you: but as the same anointing teaches you of all things, and is truth, and is no lie, and even as it hath taught you, ye shall abide in Him.

-- 1 John 2:27

Congratulations!

This is the day that you shall spring forth says the Lord of hosts.

Behold, I will do a new thing; now it shall spring forth; shall ye not know it? I will even make a way in the wilderness, and rivers in the desert.

-- Isaiah 43:19

Congratulations!

The enemy that you see now you will see no more.

And Moses said unto the people, Fear ye not, stand still, and see the salvation of the LORD, which He will shew to you today: for the Egyptians whom ye have seen today, ye shall see them again no more forever.

-- Exodus 14:1

DAY 11

Congratulations!

Your season of feeling insignificant is over.

Take a good look, friends, at who you were when you got called into this life. I don't see many of "the brightest and the best" among you, not many influential, not many from high-society families. Isn't it obvious that God deliberately chose men and women that the culture overlooks and exploits and abuses, chose these "nobodies" to expose the hollow pretensions of the "somebodies"?

-- 1Corinthians 1:28, MSG

17

Congratulations!

Enough is enough! You are about to walk into the best season of your life.

A new day will dawn on us from above because our God is loving and merciful.

-- Luke 1:78, GWT

Congratulations!

A fresh anointing is coming your way.

Jesus Christ will fill your lives with everything that God's approval produces. Your lives will then bring glory and praise to God.

See Philippians 1:9-11, KJV

Congratulations!

You are where you are supposed to be and that is where your favor lies.

You bless righteous people, O LORD. Like a large shield, You surround them with Your favor.

– Psalms 5:12, GWT

DAY 15

Congratulations!

Things are where they should be.

No eye has seen, nor ear has heard, and no mind has imagined the things that God has prepared for those who love him. God has revealed those things to us by his Spirit. The Spirit searches everything, especially the deep things of God.

-- 1 Corinthians 2:9-10, GWT

Congratulations!

You thought your well was dried up but God is about to bring new life, new waters, and an abundance of rain.

And Elijah said unto Ahab, get thee up, eat and drink; for there is a sound of abundance of rain.

-- 1 Kings 18:41 KJV

22

Congratulations!

You are about to walk into the best decisions you have ever made in your life.

They also do no iniquity: they walk in His ways.

-- Psalm 119:3

Congratulations!

Riches will abide in your house.

Wealth and riches *shall be* in his house: and his righteousness endureth forever.

– Psalm 112:3

Congratulations!

You belong to God.

Know ye that the LORD He is God: it is He that hath made us, and not we ourselves; we are His people, and the sheep of His pasture.

-- Psalm 100:3

Congratulations!

Lift up your head; greater is coming.

But thou, O LORD, *art* a shield for me; my glory, and the lifter up of mine head.

– Psalm 3:3

DAY 21

Congratulations!

Repeat: Favor, favor, favor; life, life, life!!!

In whom also we have obtained an inheritance, being predestinated according to the purpose of Him who worketh all things after the counsel of His own will:

-- Ephesians 1:11

Congratulations!

Because you have positioned yourself in the right atmosphere, what God purposed for you is about to come to pass.

I will stand upon my watch, and set me upon the tower, and will watch to see what He will say unto me, and what I shall answer when I am reproved.

-- Habakkuk 2:1

Congratulations!

While you yield, God is working things out in your life!

Neither yield ye your members as instruments of unrighteousness unto sin: but yield yourselves unto God, as those that are alive from the dead, and your members *as* instruments of righteousness unto God.

-- Roman 6:13

Congratulations!

God is performing, and exceeding your expectations... Shift!

Now unto Him that is able to do exceeding abundantly above all that we ask or think, according to the power that worketh in us…

-- Ephesians 3:20

Congratulations!

God is bigger than all your problems, your fears, or anything you can and cannot see.

For God has not given us a spirit of fear, but of power and of love and of a sound mind.

-- 2 Timothy 1:7

Congratulations!

The fiery trials that may come are not to be taken personally! They are only tests. Rejoice!

Beloved, do not be surprised at the fiery trial that has come upon you, as though something strange were happening to you. But rejoice that you share in the sufferings of Christ, so that you may be overjoyed at the revelation of His glory.
-- 1 Peter 4:12-13, BSB

DAY 27

Congratulations!

This is your hour, day, and season of visitation.

For behold, when the sound of your greeting reached my ears, the baby leaped in my womb for joy… And blessed *is* she who believed that there would be a fulfillment of what had been spoken to her by the Lord.

See Luke 1:39-45, NAS

Congratulations!

Whatever you have missed, you will see it still manifest.

"You have asked a difficult thing," Elijah said, "yet if you see me when I am taken from you, it will be yours--otherwise, it will not."

-- 2 Kings 2:10

DAY 29

Congratulations!

This will be the year you will hear more clearly than you have heard before.

While it is said, Today if ye will hear his voice, harden not your hearts, as in the provocation.

– Hebrews 3:15

Congratulations!

God is who He is

in your life.

And God said unto Moses, I AM THAT I AM: and He said, thus shalt thou say unto the children of Israel, I AM hath sent me unto you.

-- Exodus 3:14

DAY 31

Congratulations!

You are not just a survivor; you are more than a conqueror!!

Nay, in all these things we are more than conquerors through him that loved us.

-- Romans 8:37

DAY 32

Congratulations!

What was standing between you and your promise is now gone.

Fear thou not; for I am with thee: be not dismayed; for I am thy God: I will strengthen thee; yea, I will help thee; yea, I will uphold thee with the right hand of my righteousness.

-- Isaiah 41:10

DAY 33

Congratulations!

A generational alignment in your family is about to occur and you shall recover all.

But they that wait upon the LORD shall renew their strength; they shall mount up with wings as eagles; they shall run, and not be weary; and they shall walk, and not faint.

-- Isaiah 40:31

Congratulations!

You will see no defeat for God is on your side.

The LORD taketh my part with them that help me: therefore, shall I see *my desire* upon them that hate me.

-- Psalms 118:7

Congratulations!

You will be invisible to the enemy, and therefore, unstoppable.

They shall take up serpents; and if they drink any deadly thing, it shall not hurt them; they shall lay hands on the sick, and they shall recover.

– Mark 16:1

DAY 36

Congratulations!

The next chapter in your life is about to begin.

And He that sat upon the throne said, Behold, I make all things new. And He said unto me, Write: for these words are true and faithful.

-- Revelation 21:5

DAY 37

Congratulations!

God has done a great work through you.

Being confident of this very thing, that he which hath begun a good work in you will perform *it* until the day of Jesus Christ:

-- Philippians 1:6

Congratulations!

Your seed is about to change your season.

Give, and it shall be given unto you; good measure, pressed down, and shaken together, and running over, shall men give into your bosom. For with the same measure that ye mete withal it shall be measured to you again.

-- Luke 6:38

Congratulations!

It's your time, your turn, and your season.

(For he saith, I have heard thee in a time accepted, and in the day of salvation have I succored thee: behold, now *is* the accepted time; behold, now *is* the day of salvation.)

-- 2 Corinthians 6:2

Congratulations!

God is about to bless all the works of your hand.

You have made them rulers over the works of your hands you put everything under their feet all flocks and herds, and the animals of the wild, the birds in the sky, and the fish in the sea, all that swim the paths of the seas. LORD, our Lord, how majestic is your name in all the earth!

-- Psalm 8:9

DAY 41

Congratulations!

You shall lend to many nations.

Give, and it shall be given unto you; good measure, pressed down, and shaken together, and running over, shall men give into your bosom. For with the same measure that ye mete withal it shall be measured to you again.

-- Luke 6:38

Congratulations!

The glory of the Lord shall be revealed in your life.

The voice of Him that cries in the wilderness, Prepare ye the way of the LORD, make straight in the desert a highway for our God. Every valley shall be exalted, and every mountain and hill shall be made low: and the crooked shall be made straight, and the rough places plain: And the glory of the LORD shall be revealed, and all flesh shall see it together: for the mouth of the LORD hath spoken *it*.

-- Isaiah 40:3-5

Congratulations!

The Lord has made you the head; you are above your enemies.

And thou shalt not borrow. And the LORD shall make thee the head, and not the tail; and thou shalt be above only, and thou shalt not be beneath; if that thou hearken unto the commandments of the LORD thy God, which I command thee this day, to observe and to do them:

-- Deuteronomy 28:12-13

Congratulations!

There are great things in store for you today!

This *is* the day the LORD has made; We will rejoice and be glad in it.

-- Psalm 118:24, NKJV

Day 45

Congratulations!

Your gift has made room for you.

Bring ye all the tithes into the storehouse,
that there may be meat in mine house,
and prove me now herewith, saith
the LORD of hosts, if I will not open you
the windows of heaven, and pour you out
a blessing, that there shall not be room
enough to receive it.

-- Malachi 3:10

Congratulations!

You are not a carbon copy; you are the Designer's original.

I will praise thee; for I am fearfully and wonderfully made: marvelous are thy works; and that my soul knoweth right well.

-- Psalm 139:14

Congratulations!

Your faith will determine your destiny.

Now faith is the substance of things hoped for, the evidence of things not seen.

-- Hebrews 11:1

Congratulations!

Every word God has spoken over your life will come to pass.

And it shall come to pass in the last days, saith God, I will pour out of my Spirit upon all flesh: and your sons and your daughters shall prophesy, and your young men shall see visions, and your old men shall dream dreams:

-- Acts 2:17

54

DAY 49

Congratulations!

Your expectation is about to manifest.

For the earnest expectation of the creature waiteth for the manifestation of the sons of God.

– Romans 8:19

Congratulations!

Your faith will meet your anointing.

Now faith is the substance of things hoped for, the evidence of things not seen. For by it the elders obtained a good report.

-- Hebrew 11:1-2

Congratulations!

Your best days are ahead of you.

But as it is written, Eye hath not seen, nor ear heard, neither have entered into the heart of man, the things which God hath prepared for them that love Him.

-- 1 Corinthians 2:9

Congratulations!

What you have sowed in tears, you are reaping in joy.

They that sow in tears shall reap in joy.

-- Psalms 126:5

DAY 53

Congratulations!

Your presence is helping others prosper.

For I know the thoughts that I think toward you, saith the LORD, thoughts of peace, and not of evil, to give you an expected end.

-- Jeremiah 29:11

Congratulations!

The blessings of the Lord will overtake you.

And all these blessings shall come on thee, and overtake thee, if thou shalt hearken unto the voice of the LORD thy God.

-- Deuteronomy 28:2

Congratulations!

You are making the right choices.

Abraham is going to become a large and strong nation; all the nations of the world are going to find themselves blessed through him. Yes, I've settled on him as the one to train his children and future family to observe GOD's way of life, live kindly and generously and fairly, so that GOD can complete in Abraham what he promised him."

– Genesis 18:19

Congratulations!

You are abundantly supplied.

And God is able to make all grace abound toward you; that ye, always having all sufficiency in all things, may abound to every good work:

-- 2 Corinthians 9:8

Congratulations!

You will receive a hundred-fold return.

And these are they which are sown on good ground; such as hear the word, and receive it, and bring forth fruit, some thirtyfold, some sixty, and some an hundred.

-- Mark 4:20

Congratulations!

You are about to choose the best options you have ever made in your life.

Lead me, O LORD, in thy righteousness because of mine enemies; make thy way straight before my face.

-- Psalm 5:8

Congratulations!

Purposed things are being birthed through, into your spirit now.

Therefore if any man be in Christ, he is a new creature: old things are passed away; behold, all things are become new.

-- 2 Corinthians 5:17

Congratulations!

You will see victory in this battle.

And he said, Hearken ye, all Judah, and ye inhabitants of Jerusalem, and thou king Jehoshaphat, Thus saith the LORD unto you, Be not afraid nor dismayed by reason of this great multitude; for the battle is not yours, but God's.

-- 2 Chronicles 20:15

Congratulations!

You will not faint in the day of adversity.

Trust in the LORD with all thine heart; and lean not unto thine own understanding. In all thy ways acknowledge him, and he shall direct thy paths.

-- Proverbs 3:5-6

Congratulations!

You are going to remain strong.

Have not I commanded thee? Be strong and of a good courage; be not afraid, neither be thou dismayed: for the LORD thy God is with thee whithersoever thou goest.

-- Joshua 1:9

Congratulations!

Your name will go before kings, queens, and rulers.

A man's gift makes room for him, and brings him before great men.

-- Proverbs 18:16

Congratulations!

Your name is in rooms that you have not yet entered.

Now unto him that is able to do exceeding abundantly above all that we ask or think, according to the power that worketh in us, Unto him be glory in the church by Christ Jesus throughout all ages, world without end. Amen.

-- Ephesians 3:20-21

Congratulations!

Your name will be in the Lamb's book of life.

But nothing unclean will ever enter it [the New Jerusalem on the New Earth], nor anyone who does what is detestable or false, but only those who are written in the Lamb's book of life

-- Revelations 21:27, CSB

Congratulations!

Greater days are ahead of you.

In the day of prosperity be joyful, but in the day of adversity consider: God also hath set the one over against the other, to the end that man should find nothing after him.

-- Ecclesiastes 7:14

Congratulations!

Supernatural blessings are on the way.

Blessed is the man that trusts in the LORD, and whose hope the LORD is. For he shall be as a tree planted by the waters, and that spreads out her roots by the river, and shall not see when heat cometh, but her leaf shall be green; and shall not be careful in the year of drought, neither shall cease from yielding fruit.

-- Jeremiah 17:7-8

Congratulations!

You will introduce people to God that do not know Him.

Then Peter said, Silver and gold have I none; but such as I have give I thee: In the name of Jesus Christ of Nazareth rise up and walk.

-- Acts 3:6

Congratulations!

Breakthrough is in your home.

Wherefore take unto you the whole armor of God, that ye may be able to withstand in the evil day, and having done all, to stand.

– Ephesians 6:13

Congratulations!

You will experience a breakthrough in your finances.

But without faith it is impossible to please Him: for He that cometh to God must believe that He is, and that He is a rewarder of them that diligently seek Him.

-- Hebrews 11:6

Congratulations!

You will experience a breakthrough in your career.

And Jesus said unto them, Because of your unbelief: for verily I say unto you, If ye have faith as a grain of mustard seed, ye shall say unto this mountain, Remove hence to yonder place; and it shall remove; and nothing shall be impossible unto you.

-- Matthew 17:20

Congratulations!

You will experience a breakthrough in your health.

Beloved, I wish above all things that thou mayest prosper and be in health, even as thy soul prospereth.

-- 3 John 2

Congratulations!

God is leaning in your direction.

Trust in the LORD with all thine heart; and lean not unto thine own understanding. In all thy ways acknowledge him, and he shall direct thy paths.

-- Proverbs 3:5-6

Congratulations!

Wealth and abundance are in your house.

And the ark of the LORD continued in the house of Obededom the Gittite three months: and the LORD blessed Obededom, and all his household.

-- 2 Samuels 6:11

Congratulations!

Your favor will fall like rain.

Be glad then, ye children of Zion, and rejoice in the LORD your God: for He hath given you the former rain moderately, and He will cause to come down for you the rain, the former rain, and the latter rain in the first month.

– Joel 2:23

Congratulations!

There shall be delay no longer.

For I am the LORD: I will speak, and the word that I shall speak shall come to pass; it shall be no more prolonged: for in your days, O rebellious house, will I say the word, and will perform it, saith the LORD GOD.

-- Ezekiel 12:25

Congratulations!

Things are starting to happen quickly.

Then Jesus answered and said unto her, O woman, great is thy faith: be it unto thee even as thou wilt. And her daughter was made whole from that very hour.

-- Matthew 15:28

Congratulations!

The purpose and plan of God are accelerating in your life.

And in very deed for this cause have I raised thee up, for to shew in thee My power; and that My name may be declared throughout all the earth.

-- Exodus 9:16

Congratulations!

Things shall begin to manifest suddenly.

If God be glorified in him, God shall also glorify him in himself, and shall straightway glorify him.

-- John 13:32

Congratulations!

Immediate good things are happening for you NOW!

Now faith is the substance of things hoped for, the evidence of things not seen.

-- Hebrew 11:1

Congratulations!

You have supernatural favor.

Surely the Lord GOD will do nothing, but He revealeth His secret unto His servants the prophets.

-- Amos 3:7

Day 82

Congratulations!

Your seed is an act of faith.

Therefore it is of faith, that it might be by grace; to the end the promise might be sure to all the **seed**; not to that only which is of the law, but to that also which is of the faith of Abraham; who is the father of us all,

-- Romans 4:16

DAY 83

Congratulations!

God will not forget His promises to you.

The Lord is not slack concerning His promise, as some men count slackness; but is longsuffering to us-ward, not willing that any should perish, but that all should come to repentance.

-- 2 Peter 3:9

Congratulations!

God is over it all.

Our God gives you everything you need, makes you everything you're to be. You need to know, friends, that thanking God over and over for you is not only a pleasure; it's a must.

-- 2 Thessalonians 1:2-3 (MSG)

Congratulations!

God has ordered your steps.

The steps of a good man are ordered by the LORD: and He delights in his way.

-- Psalm 37:23

Congratulations!

It's not over until God says it's over.

Behold, we go up to Jerusalem; and the Son of man shall be betrayed unto the chief priests and unto the scribes, and they shall condemn Him to death, And shall deliver Him to the Gentiles to mock, and to scourge, and to crucify Him: and the third day He shall rise again.

-- Matthew 20:18-19

Congratulations!

You are operating in divine dominion.

Far above all principality, and power, and might, and dominion, and every name that is named, not only in this world, but also in that which is to come.

-- Ephesians 1:21

Congratulations!

You are operating in your anointing.

Thou preparest a table before me in the presence of mine enemies: thou anointest my head with oil; my cup runneth over.

-- Psalm 23:5

Congratulations!

You are operating in rulership.

And the kingdom and dominion, and the greatness of the kingdom under the whole heaven, shall be given to the people of the saints of the most High, whose kingdom is an everlasting kingdom, and all dominions shall serve and obey him.

-- Daniel 7:27

DAY 90

Congratulations!

Your sick family members will be healed.

And said, If thou wilt diligently hearken to the voice of the LORD thy God, and wilt do that which is right in his sight, and wilt give ear to his commandments, and keep all his statutes, I will put none of these diseases upon thee, which I have brought upon the Egyptians: for I am the LORD that healeth thee.

-- Exodus 15:26

Congratulations!

There will be mending for broken relationships.

Casting all your care upon Him; for He cares for you.

-- 1 Peter 5:7

Congratulations!

You will have the finance for debt consolidation.

At the end of every seven years thou shalt make a release.

-- Deuteronomy 15:1

Congratulations!

You are in line for a promotion.

For promotion cometh neither from the east, nor from the west, nor from the south. But God is the judge: he putteth down one, and setteth up another.

-- Psalm 75:6-7

Congratulations!

Your children will appreciate what you do.

Honor thy father and thy mother: that thy days may be long upon the land which the LORD thy God giveth thee.

-- Exodus 20:12

Congratulations!

The peace of Christ will begin to rule in your heart.

And let the peace of God rule in your hearts, to the which also ye are called in one body; and be ye thankful.

– Colossians 3:15

Congratulations!

You will know God's voice.

Also I heard the voice of the Lord, saying, Whom shall I send, and who will go for us? Then said I, Here *am* I; send me.

-- Isaiah 6:8

Day 97

Congratulations!

You will maintain the blessing of God in your life.

The blessing of the LORD, it maketh rich, and he addeth no sorrow with it.

-- Proverbs 10:22

Congratulations!

Christ dwells in you.

Whereof I was made a minister, according to the gift of the grace of God given unto me by the effectual working of His power.

– Ephesians 3:7

Congratulations!

The angels of the Lord are encamped around you.

The angel of the LORD encampeth round about them that fear him, and delivereth them.

– Psalm 34:7

Congratulations!

The angels of Lord are delivering you because you fear the Lord.

The fear of the LORD is the beginning of wisdom: and the knowledge of the holy is understanding.

-- Proverbs 9:10

Congratulations!

You are one of Christ's anointed.

Now he which stablisheth us with you in Christ, and hath anointed us, is God;

– 2 Corinthians 1:21

Congratulations!

You are moving from transition to manifestation.

For the earnest expectation of the creature waiteth for the manifestation of the sons of God.

– Romans 8:19

Congratulations!

You will recover all and fear no evil.

Yea, though I walk through the valley of the shadow of death, I will fear no evil: for thou art with me; thy rod and thy staff they comfort me.

-- Psalm 23:4

DAY 104

Congratulations!

Every evil hand pointed at your destiny this year must wither and die.

And he shall be like a tree planted by the rivers of water, that bringeth forth his fruit in his season; his leaf also shall not wither; and whatsoever he doeth shall prosper.

– Psalm 1:3

110

DAY 105

Congratulations!

Your Redeemer lives despite trials and tribulations.

Looking at it one way, you could say, "Anything goes. Because of God's immense generosity and grace, we don't have to dissect and scrutinize every action to see if it will pass muster." But the point is not to just get by. We want to live well, but our foremost efforts should be to help *others* live well.

-- 1 Corinthians 10:23, MSG

Congratulations!

You are hereby acquitted of the mistakes of your past.

For all have sinned, and come short of the glory of God; Being justified freely by His grace through the redemption that is in Christ Jesus:

– Romans 3:22-24

Congratulations!

Nothing has an advantage over you; you are in the clear.

Ye shall not therefore oppress one another; but thou shalt fear thy God: for I am the LORD your God.

-- Leviticus 25:17

Congratulations!

You have dominion over all that has been put under your charge.

And God said, Let us make man in our image, after our likeness: and let them have dominion over the fish of the sea, and over the fowl of the air, and over the cattle, and over all the earth, and over every creeping thing that creepeth upon the earth.

– Genesis 1:26

Congratulations!

You are blessed with love.

Love endures with patience *and* serenity, love is kind *and* thoughtful, and is not jealous *or* envious; love does not brag and is not proud *or* arrogant.

-- 1 Corinthians 13:4, AMP

Congratulations!

You will have God-given guidance.

I will instruct you and teach you in the way you should go; I will counsel you [who are willing to learn] with My eye upon you.

– Psalm 32:8

Congratulations!

The right people will come into your life.

There hath no temptation taken you but such as is common to man: but God is faithful, who will not suffer you to be tempted above that ye are able; but will with the temptation also make a way to escape, that ye may be able to bear it.

-- 1 Corinthians 10:13

DAY 112

Congratulations!

You will have peace and rest.

He gives power to the weak, And to *those who have* no might He increases strength.

-- Isaiah 40:29, NKJV

Congratulations!

New opportunities are coming your way in Jesus' name.

Therefore if any man be in Christ, he is a new creature: old things are passed away; behold, all things are become new.

-- 2 Corinthians 5:17

DAY 114

Congratulations!

No drama will come your way.

No weapon that is formed against thee shall prosper; and every tongue that shall rise against thee in judgment thou shalt condemn. This is the heritage of the servants of the LORD, and their righteousness is of me, saith the LORD.

-- Isaiah 54:17

DAY 115

Congratulations!

You will keep yourself out of arguments.

That you also aspire to lead a quiet life, to mind your own business, and to work with your own hands, as we commanded you,

-- 1 Thessalonians 4:11, NKJV

Congratulations!

The Spirit of God is seizing the lack in your life.

For the LORD thy God hath blessed thee in all the works of thy hand: he knoweth thy walking through this great wilderness: these forty years the LORD thy God hath been with thee; thou hast lacked nothing.

-- Deuteronomy 2:7

Congratulations!

The Spirit of God is seizing the poverty in your life.

The LORD shall open unto thee His good treasure, the heaven to give the rain unto thy land in his season, and to bless all the work of thine hand: and thou shalt lend unto many nations, and thou shalt not borrow.

-- Deuteronomy 28:12

Congratulations!

The Spirit of God is seizing the inconsistency in your life.

The Lord is not slack concerning his promise, as some men count slackness; but is longsuffering to us-ward, not willing that any should perish, but that all should come to repentance.

– 2 Peter 3:9

Congratulations!

Fresh revelation is being released upon you.

But God hath revealed them unto us by his Spirit: for the Spirit searcheth all things, yea, the deep things of God.

-- 1 Corinthians 2:10

Congratulations!

You will walk into the fullness of your breakthrough.

Thou wilt shew me the path of life: in thy presence is fulness of joy; at thy right hand there are pleasures for evermore.

– Psalm 16:11

Congratulations!

You are in a time-processing season.

Behold, I have refined you, but not as silver; I have tested you in the furnace of affliction. For My own sake, for My own sake, I will do *it;*

-- Isaiah 48:10-11a

DAY 122

Congratulations!

You have an expected end.

For I know the thoughts that I think toward you, saith the LORD, thoughts of peace, and not of evil, to give you an expected end.

– Jeremiah 29:11

DAY 123

Congratulations!

There is a next for you.

Being confident of this very thing, that he which hath begun a good work in you will perform it until the day of Jesus Christ:

-- Philippians 1:6

Congratulations!

Where you are, is temporary.

And God will wipe away every tear from their eyes; there shall be no more death, nor sorrow, nor crying. There shall be no more pain, for the former things have passed away.

-- Revelation 21:4

Congratulations!

What God has for you is bigger than your now!

Ye are of God, little children, and have overcome them: because greater is He that is in you, than he that is in the world.

– 1 John 4:4

Congratulations!

Great things are happening for you.

The Lord hath done great things for us; whereof we are glad.

– Psalm 126:3

Congratulations!

You are outside of time and you are inside the mind of God.

For "who has known the mind of the LORD that he may instruct Him?" But we have the mind of Christ.

-- 1 Corinthians 2:16, NKJV

Congratulations!

Your faith is the passion for the possible.

Now faith is the substance of things hoped for, the evidence of things not seen.

-- Hebrews 11:1

Congratulations!

Your obedience will produce blessings.

And I will make thy seed to multiply as the stars of heaven, and will give unto thy seed all these countries; and in thy seed shall all the nations of the earth be blessed; Because that Abraham obeyed my voice, and kept my charge, my commandments, my statutes, and my laws.

-- Genesis 26:4-5

Congratulations!

Whatever you have been thinking is too small; think greater.

Eye has not seen, nor ear heard, nor have entered into the heart of man. The things which God has prepared for those who love Him.

-- 1 Corinthians 2:9, NKJV

Congratulations!

God will do more than He did yesterday.

Now the God of peace, that brought again from the dead our Lord Jesus, that great Shepherd of the sheep, through the blood of the everlasting covenant, Make you perfect in every good work to do His will, working in you that which is well-pleasing in His sight, through Jesus Christ; to whom be glory for ever and ever. Amen.

-- Hebrews 13:20-21

Congratulations!

The Lord will increase you and your children.

Not unto us, O LORD, not unto us, but unto thy name give glory, for thy mercy, and for thy truth's sake.

-- Psalm 115:1

Congratulations!

God has greater plans.

Then shall ye call upon me, and ye shall go and pray unto me, and I will hearken unto you.

-- Jeremiah 29:12

Congratulations!

The Lord will open to you His good pleasures.

Thou wilt shew me the path of life: in thy presence *is* fulness of joy; at thy right hand *there are* pleasures for evermore.

-- Psalm 16:11

Congratulations!

You shall receive prosperity in all areas of your heart's desires.

Delight yourself also in the LORD, And He shall give you the desires of your heart.

-- Psalm 37:4

Congratulations!

The promises are yes and amen.

For all the promises of God in him are yea, and in him Amen, unto the glory of God by us.

-- 2 Corinthians 1:20

Congratulations!

You have what you say.

For verily I say unto you, That whosoever shall say unto this mountain, Be thou removed, and be thou cast into the sea; and shall not doubt in his heart, but shall believe that those things which he saith shall come to pass; he shall have whatsoever he saith.

-- Mark 11:23

Congratulations!

Have no doubt in your mind that God will answer your prayer.

If any of you lack wisdom, let him ask of God, that giveth to all men liberally, and upbraideth not; and it shall be given him.

-- James 1:5-8

Congratulations!

God will give you whatever you ask.

Ask, and it shall be given you; seek, and ye shall find; knock, and it shall be opened unto you: For every one that asketh receiveth; and he that seeketh findeth; and to him that knocketh it shall be opened.

-- Matthew 7:7-8

Congratulations!

You are receiving an abundance of miracles.

So she left him, and after she had shut the door behind her and her sons, they kept bringing jars to her, and she kept pouring. When all the jars were full, she said to her son, "Bring me another." But he replied, "There is not a jar left." Then the oil stopped flowing. She went and told the man of God, and he said, "Go, sell the oil and pay your debts. You and your sons can live on what is left."

-- 2 Kings 4:5-7, NIV

Congratulations!

You've survived 100% of what you've been through.

Make a joyful noise unto the LORD, all ye lands.

-- Psalm 100:1

Congratulations!

There shall be delay no longer.

But they that wait upon the LORD shall renew their strength; they shall mount up with wings as eagles; they shall run, and not be weary; and they shall walk, and not faint.

-- Isaiah 40:31

Congratulations!

God is ADONAI, the LORD your Master.

For by Him were all things created, that are in heaven, and that are in earth, visible and invisible, whether they be thrones, or dominions, or principalities, or powers: all things were created by Him, and for Him:

-- Colossians 1:16

Congratulations!

You are operating within divine power.

Far above all principality, and power, and might, and dominion, and every name that is named, not only in this world, but also in that which is to come:

-- Ephesians 1:21

Congratulations!

God is Jehovah Jireh; He will provide for you.

And Abraham lifted up his eyes, and looked, and behold behind him a ram caught in a thicket by his horns: and Abraham went and took the ram, and offered him up for a burnt offering in the stead of his son.

-- Genesis 22:13

Congratulations!

God is Jehovah Rapha, the LORD that heals you.

And said, If thou wilt diligently hearken to the voice of the LORD thy God, and wilt do that which is right in his sight, and wilt give ear to his commandments, and keep all his statutes, I will put none of these diseases upon thee, which I have brought upon the Egyptians: for I am the LORD that healeth thee.

-- Exodus 15:26

Congratulations!

God is Jehovah Shammah, the LORD who is present with you.

It was round about eighteen thousand measures: and the name of the city from that day shall be, The LORD is there.

-- Ezekiel 48:35

DAY 148

Congratulations!

God is Jehovah Shalom, the LORD your peace.

So Gideon built an altar to the LORD there and called it The LORD Is Peace…

-- Judges 6:24

Peace I leave with you, My peace I give to you; not as the world gives do I give to you. Let not your heart be troubled, neither let it be afraid.

-- John 14:27, NKJV

Congratulations!

God is Jehovah Nissi, the LORD your banner. He will fight for you.

And the LORD said unto Moses, Write this for a memorial in a book, and rehearse it in the ears of Joshua: for I will utterly put out the remembrance of Amalek from under heaven. And Moses built an altar, and called the name of it Jehovah-nissi: For he said, Because the LORD hath sworn that the LORD will have war with Amalek from generation to generation.

-- Exodus 17:14-16

155

Congratulations!

God is Jehovah Raah, the LORD your shepherd, who cares for you, His sheep.

The LORD is my shepherd; I shall not want.

-- Psalm 23:1

Congratulations!

God is Jehovah Tsidkenu, the LORD your righteousness.

In His days Judah shall be saved, and Israel shall dwell safely: and this is His name whereby He shall be called, THE LORD OUR RIGHTEOUSNESS.

-- Jeremiah 23:6

Congratulations!

God is El Shaddai, the LORD God Almighty. He will make your name great.

And God said unto him, I am God Almighty: be fruitful and multiply; a nation and a company of nations shall be of thee, and kings shall come out of thy loins;

-- Genesis 35:11

Congratulations!

God is El Elyon, the LORD most high God. You are blessed of Him.

And he blessed him, and said, Blessed be Abram of the most high God, possessor of heaven and earth:

– Genesis 14:19

Congratulations!

God will replace that which you have lost.

And I will restore to you the years that the locust hath eaten, the cankerworm, and the caterpillar, and the palmerworm, my great army which I sent among you.

-- Joel 2:25

Congratulations!

Your God is Yahweh, the LORD and Jehovah.

For I know that Yahweh is great, that our Lord is above all gods.

-- Psalm 135:5

Congratulations!

God is Jehovah Mekoddishkem, He who sanctifies you.

Speak thou also unto the children of Israel, saying, Verily my Sabbaths ye shall keep: for it is a sign between me and you throughout your generations; that ye may know that I am the LORD that doth sanctify you.

-- Exodus 31:13

Congratulations!

Your God is Elohim, the one true and living God.

So do not fear, for I am with you; do not be dismayed, for **I am your God**. I will strengthen you and help you; I will uphold you with my righteous right hand.

-- Isaiah 41:10, NIV

Congratulations!

Your God is El Olam, the everlasting God. He will be forever, and is forever with you.

But the mercy of the LORD is from everlasting to everlasting upon them that fear Him, and His righteousness unto children's children;

-- Psalm 103:17

Congratulations!

God is Qanna, Jealous. He is jealous for you and will not share you with another.

For thou shalt worship no other god: for the LORD, whose name is Jealous, is a jealous God:

– Exodus 34:14

Congratulations!

God is giving you strength for your day.

I can do all things through Christ which strengtheneth me.

– Philippians 4:13

Congratulations!

God has established your plans.

Commit thy works unto the LORD, and thy thoughts shall be established.

-- Proverbs 16:3

Congratulations!

God will make you successful and bless your household.

And it came to pass from the time that he had made him overseer in his house, and over all that he had, that the LORD blessed the Egyptian's house for Joseph's sake; and the blessing of the LORD was upon all that he had in the house, and in the field.

-- Genesis 39:5

DAY 163

Congratulations!

You will flourish wherever you go.

And keep the charge of the LORD thy God, to walk in his ways, to keep his statutes, and his commandments, and his judgments, and his testimonies, as it is written in the law of Moses, that thou mayest prosper in all that thou doest, and whithersoever thou turnest thyself:

-- 1 Kings 2:3

Congratulations!

The next move will bring you the peace for which you have prayed.

And the peace of God, which passeth all understanding, shall keep your hearts and minds through Christ Jesus

-- Philippians 4:7

Congratulations!

You have no need to be anxious for anything.

Be careful for nothing; but in everything by prayer and supplication with thanksgiving let your requests be made known unto God.

-- Philippians 4:6

Congratulations!

You will produce great wealth.

But thou shalt remember the LORD thy God: for it is He that giveth thee power to get wealth, that He may establish His covenant which He sware unto thy fathers, as it is this day.

-- Deuteronomy 8:18

Congratulations!

God will make you to know His path for your life.

I will bless the LORD, who hath given me counsel: my reins also instruct me in the night seasons.

-- Psalm 16:7-11

Congratulations!

God will keep you in perfect peace.

Thou wilt keep him in perfect peace, whose mind is stayed on thee: because he trusteth in Thee. Trust ye in the LORD forever: for in the LORD JEHOVAH is everlasting strength:

-- Isaiah 26:3-4

174

Congratulations!

God will make you blameless.

Who shall also confirm you unto the end, that ye may be blameless in the day of our Lord Jesus Christ .God is faithful, by whom ye were called unto the fellowship of his Son Jesus Christ our Lord.

-- 1 Corinthians 1:8-9

Congratulations!

God will give you instruction.

Hear, ye children, the instruction of a father, and attend to know understanding.

-- Proverbs 4:1-2

Congratulations!

Wisdom will be like honey for you.

So shall the knowledge of wisdom be unto thy soul: when thou hast found it, then there shall be a reward, and thy expectation shall not be cut off.

-- Proverbs 24:14

Congratulations!

May the LORD bless you and keep you.

The LORD bless thee, and keep
thee: The LORD make his face shine upon
thee, and be gracious unto thee:
The LORD lift up his countenance upon
thee, and give thee peace.

-- Numbers 6:24-26

Congratulations!

God will give you insight, witty ideas, and creative inventions.

See, I have called by name Bezalel …And I have filled him with the Spirit of God, in wisdom, in understanding, in knowledge, and in all *manner of* workmanship, to design artistic works, to work in gold, in silver, in bronze, in cutting jewels for setting, in carving wood, and to work in all *manner of* workmanship.

-- Exodus 31:2-5, NKJV

179

DAY 174

Congratulations!

You will seek Me and find Me, when you seek Me with all your heart.

And ye shall seek me, and find me, when ye shall search for me with all your heart.

-- Jeremiah 29:13

Congratulations!

God formed your inward parts; God knitted you together in your mother's womb.

For thou hast possessed my reins: thou hast covered me in my mother's womb.

-- Psalm 139:13

Congratulations!

Behold, the children in your family are gifts from the LORD.

Lo, children are an heritage of the LORD: and the fruit of the womb is his reward.

-- Psalm 127:3

Congratulations!

God's word is a lamp to your feet to keep you on the right path.

Thy word is a lamp unto my feet, and a light unto my path.

-- Psalm 119:105

Congratulations!

You are strong and courageous.

Be strong and of a good courage, fear not, nor be afraid of them: for the LORD thy God, He it is that doth go with thee; He will not fail thee, nor forsake thee.

– Deuteronomy 31:6

Congratulations!

Your best life will not include the worst of your past.

I press toward the mark for the prize of the high calling of God in Christ Jesus.

-- Philippians 3:14

Congratulations!

You will walk in God's delight.

Blessed is the man that walketh not in the counsel of the ungodly, nor standeth in the way of sinners, nor sitteth in the seat of the scornful. But his delight is in the law of the LORD; and in His law doth he meditate day and night.

-- Psalm 1:1

Congratulations!

You are generous and you will be prosperous.

The liberal soul shall be made fat: and he that watereth shall be watered also himself.

-- Proverbs 11:25

DAY 182

Congratulations!

God will be faithful to you.

God is faithful, by whom you were called into the fellowship of his Son, Jesus Christ our Lord.

-- 1 Corinthians 1:9

Congratulations!

You will find peace as you think on these things.

Finally, brethren, whatever things are true, whatever things *are* noble, whatever things *are* just, whatever things *are* pure, whatever things *are* lovely, whatever things *are* of good report, if *there is* any virtue and if *there is* anything praiseworthy —meditate on these things.

-- Philippians 4:8, NKJV

Congratulations!

God is your refuge and strength.

God is our refuge and strength, a very present help in trouble.

-- Psalm 46:1

DAY 185

Congratulations!

You are one idea away from your success.

For we are His workmanship, created in Christ Jesus unto good works, which God hath before ordained that we should walk in them.

-- Ephesians 2:10

Congratulations!

It is the LORD your God who goes with you.

Be strong and of good courage, do not fear nor be afraid of them; for the LORD your God, He *Is* the One who goes with you. He will not leave you nor forsake you.

– Deuteronomy 31:6

Congratulations!

The Lord is your portion.

The LORD *is* my portion, saith my soul; therefore will I hope in him.

-- Lamentations 3:24

Congratulations!

You will not be overcome by evil.

Nay, in all these things we are more than conquerors through him that loved us.

-- Romans 8:37

Congratulations!

You will endure.

No temptation has overtaken you but such as is common to man; and God is faithful, who will not allow you to be tempted beyond what you are able, but with the temptation will provide the way of escape also, so that you will be able to endure it.

-- 1 Corinthians 10:13, NASB

Congratulations!

In deep water God will be with you.

When you pass through the waters, I *will be* with you; And through the rivers, they shall not overflow you. When you walk through the fire, you shall not be burned, Nor shall the flame scorch you.

-- Isaiah 43:2, NKJV

Congratulations!

You have sinned, but you are free by the grace of God.

For all have sinned and fall short of the glory of God being justified freely by His grace through the redemption that is in Christ Jesus,

-- Romans 3:23-24, NKJV

DAY 192

Congratulations!

God can keep you from falling.

Now unto Him that is able to keep you from falling, and to present you faultless before the presence of His glory with exceeding joy,

– Jude 24:1

Congratulations!

You have an eternal place.

Let not your heart be troubled; you believe in God, believe also in Me. In My Father's house are many mansions; if *it were* not *so,* I would have told you. I go to prepare a place for you.

-- John 14:1-2, NKJV

Congratulations!

As you walk with Him, you are walking in the Light.

This is the message which we have heard from Him and declare to you, that God is light and in Him is no darkness at all.

-- 1 John 1:5 KJV

Congratulations!

God is putting people in your path to propel you forward.

Then Jonathan and David made a covenant, because he loved him as his own soul.

-- 1 Samuel 18:3

Congratulations!

You are stepping into greater increase.

Enlarge the place of your tent, And let them stretch out the curtains of your dwellings; Do not spare; Lengthen your cords, And strengthen your stakes.

-- Isaiah 54:2, NKJV

Congratulations!

Circumstances tried to rob you but did not succeed.

Stand fast therefore in the liberty by which Christ has made us free, and do not be entangled again with a yoke of bondage.

– Galatians 5:1, NKJV

Congratulations!

The prophetic word over your life is being manifested.

And all these blessings shall come upon you and overtake you, because you obey the voice of the LORD your God:

– Deuteronomy 28:1

DAY 199

Congratulations!

You can be courageous.

Watch, stand fast in the faith, be brave, be strong. Let all *that* you *do* be done with love.

-- 1 Corinthians 16:13-14, NKJV

Congratulations!

You are being freed from people.

Therefore if the Son makes you free, you shall be free indeed.

-- John 8:36, NKJV

Congratulations!

Your destiny is within reach.

So shall my word be that goeth forth out of my mouth: it shall not return unto me void, but it shall accomplish that which I please, and it shall prosper in the thing whereto I sent it.

– Isaiah 55:11

Congratulations!

The power of your transformed thoughts are paving a new way of being in the world.

And be not conformed to this world: but be ye transformed by the renewing of your mind, that ye may prove what is that good, and acceptable, and perfect, will of God.

-- Romans 12:2

Congratulations!

The strength of your prayers has made the difference in your family.

Confess your faults one to another, and pray one for another, that ye may be healed. The effectual fervent prayer of a righteous man availeth much.

-- James 5:16

Congratulations!

Your loved ones are coming to Christ simply because you did not give up.

For God is not unrighteous to forget your work and labor of love, which ye have shewed toward His name, in that ye have ministered to the saints, and do minister.

-- Hebrews 6:10

Congratulations!

When the dust settles you will arise.

And whosoever shall not receive you, nor hear your words, when ye depart out of that house or city, shake off the dust of your feet.

-- Matthew 10:14

Congratulations!

When you keep pushing and praying, God is pleased.

I will therefore that men pray everywhere, lifting up holy hands, without wrath and doubting.

-- 1 Timothy 2:8

Congratulations!

Your bold acts have kept the enemy at bay.

And the LORD said unto Satan, The LORD rebuke thee, O Satan; even the LORD that hath chosen Jerusalem rebuke thee: is not this a brand plucked out of the fire?

-- Zechariah 3:2

Congratulations!

It's your 20/20 season to be established and prosperous.

Believe in the LORD your God, so shall ye be established; believe his prophets, so shall ye prosper.

-- 2 Chronicles 20:20

Congratulations!

You will no longer battle back and forth with lack of resources.

But my God shall supply all your need according to his riches in glory by Christ Jesus.

– Philippians 4:19

Congratulations!

Salvation and healing go hand in hand.

Bless the LORD, O my soul: and all that is within me, bless His holy name. Bless the LORD, O my soul, and forget not all His benefits: Who forgives all thine iniquities; who heals all thy diseases;

-- Psalm 103:1-3

Congratulations!

Your anointing is the curse-breaker.

And it shall come to pass in that day, that his burden shall be taken away from off thy shoulder, and his yoke from off thy neck, and the yoke shall be destroyed because of the anointing.

-- Isaiah 10:27

Congratulations!

You are about to triumph.

Rejoice not against me, O mine enemy: when I fall, I shall arise; when I sit in darkness, the LORD shall be a light unto me.

-- Micah 7:8

DAY 213

Congratulations!

God is about to perfect and mature you.

The LORD will perfect that which concerns me: thy mercy, O LORD, endures forever: forsake not the works of thine own hands.

-- Psalm 138:8

Congratulations!

You have the faith of Abraham and will be rewarded for it.

And he brought him forth abroad, and said, Look now toward heaven, and tell the stars, if thou be able to number them: and he said unto him, So shall thy seed be.

-- Genesis 15:5

DAY 215

Congratulations!

The LORD will shine upon you and your circumstances.

The LORD bless thee, and keep thee: The LORD make his face shine upon thee, and be gracious unto thee: The LORD lift up his countenance upon thee, and give thee peace.

-- Numbers 6:24-26

Congratulations!

You can decree what you want to come to pass.

Thou shalt also decree a thing, and it shall be established unto thee: and the light shall shine upon thy ways.

-- Job 22:28

Congratulations!

Your victory is incontestable.

O death, where is thy sting? O grave, where is thy victory? The sting of death is sin; and the strength of sin is the law. But thanks be to God, which giveth us the victory through our Lord Jesus Christ.

-- 1 Corinthians 15:55-57

Congratulations!

You have the boldness of Rahab.

And the king of Jericho sent unto Rahab, saying, Bring forth the men that are come to thee, which are entered into thine house: for they be come to search out all the country. Then the woman took the two men and hid them.

-- Joshua 2:3-4a

Congratulations!

GOD is unbeatable.
God is on your side.
YOU are unbeatable.

And the Lord said unto Joshua, Fear them not: for I have delivered them into thine hand; there shall not a man of them stand before thee.

-- Joshua 10:8

DAY 220

Congratulations!

Your next step is UP!

And let us not be weary in well doing: for in due season we shall reap, if we faint not.

-- Galatians 6:9

Congratulations!

You have the authority to move every mountain.

For verily I say unto you, That whosoever shall say unto this mountain, Be thou removed, and be thou cast into the sea; and shall not doubt in his heart, but shall believe that those things which he saith shall come to pass; he shall have whatsoever he saith.

-- Mark 11:23

227

DAY 222

Congratulations!

You have the power to take what is yours.

And the LORD thy God will bring thee into the land which thy fathers possessed, and thou shalt possess it; and He will do thee good, and multiply thee above thy fathers.

-- Deuteronomy 30:5

Congratulations!

You have the strength to withstand any situation.

Therefore, my beloved brethren, be ye steadfast, unmovable, always abounding in the work of the Lord, forasmuch as ye know that your labor is not in vain in the Lord.

— 1 Corinthians 15:58

Congratulations!

You will have the promotion of Joseph.

And Pharaoh took off his ring from his hand, and put it upon Joseph's hand, and arrayed him in vestures of fine linen, and put a gold chain about his neck;

-- Genesis 41:42

Congratulations!

No attack can stop you.

No weapon that is formed against thee shall prosper; and every tongue that shall rise against thee in judgment thou shalt condemn. This is the heritage of the servants of the LORD, and their righteousness is of me, saith the LORD.

– Isaiah 54:17

Congratulations!

This is your time. God is removing everything that is weighing you down.

Come unto me, all *ye* that labor and are heavy laden, and I will give you rest.

-- Matthew 11:28

Congratulations!

You are about to transition into your next chapter of greatness.

And with great power gave the apostles witness of the resurrection of the LORD Jesus: and great grace was upon them all.

-- Acts 4:33

Congratulations!

You are the answer for whom someone is praying.

The administration of this service not only supplies the needs of the saints, but also is abounding through many thanksgivings to God.

-- 2 Corinthians 9:12, NKJV

Congratulations!

Your tongue holds more power than you think.

Death and life are in the power of the tongue: and they that love it shall eat the fruit thereof.

-- Proverbs 18:21

Congratulations!

You are undefeatable!

For whatever is born of God overcomes the world. And this is the victory that has overcome the world—our faith.

– 1 John 5:4, NKJV

Congratulations!

You have the oil that they need.

Thou hast loved righteousness, and hated iniquity; therefore God, even thy God, hath anointed thee with the oil of gladness above thy fellows.

– Hebrews 1:9

Congratulations!

Your God is the one and only King of kings and the Lord of lords.

Which in His times He shall shew, who is the blessed and only Potentate, the King of kings, and Lord of lords;

-- 1 Timothy 6:15

Congratulations!

Prayer will catapult you into accessing greater levels of economic and directional potential.

Pray without ceasing. In everything give thanks: for this is the will of God in Christ Jesus concerning you.

-- I Thessalonians 5:17-18

Congratulations!

What God has for you is for you.

A good man leaveth an inheritance to his children's children: and the wealth of the sinner is laid up for the just.

-- Proverbs 13:22

Congratulations!

You are defeating the work of the enemy with the Word of God.

The LORD shall cause thine enemies that rise up against thee to be smitten before thy face: they shall come out against thee one way, and flee before thee seven ways.

-- Deuteronomy 28:7

Congratulations!

Your vision is unobstructed.

For now we see through a glass, darkly; but then face to face: now I know in part; but then shall I know even as also I am known.

-- 1 Corinthians 13:12

Congratulations!

The Lord is releasing a fresh new air of peace around you to eliminate the noise.

Peace I leave with you, my peace I give unto you: not as the world giveth, give I unto you. Let not your heart be troubled, neither let it be afraid.

-- John 14:27

Congratulations!

You will rise above every disappointment.

For my thoughts are not your thoughts, neither are your ways my ways, saith the LORD. For as the heavens are higher than the earth, so are my ways higher than your ways, and my thoughts than your thoughts.

– Isaiah 55:8-9

Congratulations!

Assemble your team; it's time for the next level of victory.

David therefore departed…and when his brethren and all his father's house heard it, they…and every one that was in distress, and every one that was in debt, and every one that was discontented, gathered themselves unto him; and he became a captain over them: and there were with him about four hundred men.

-- 1 Samuel 22:1-2

Congratulations!

Your mistakes are not being held against you.

But God commendeth His love toward us, in that, while we were yet sinners, Christ died for us.

-- Romans 5:8

Congratulations!

You will begin to emerge and gradually become conspicuous.

But He knoweth the way that I take: when He hath tried me, I shall come forth as gold.

-- Job 23:10

Congratulations!

You are removing every disempowering feeling.

That ye put off concerning the former conversation the old man, which is corrupt according to the deceitful lusts; And be renewed in the spirit of your mind;

-- Ephesians 4:22-23

Congratulations!

You can tell the destroyer to get under your feet.

And the God of peace will crush Satan under your feet shortly.

– Romans 16:20a

DAY 244

Congratulations!

Your afflictions will not hold you back.

But he was wounded for our transgressions, he was bruised for our iniquities: the chastisement of our peace was upon him; and with his stripes we are healed.

-- Isaiah 53:5

Congratulations!

Your success is undeniable!

Though I walk in the midst of trouble, thou wilt revive me: thou shalt stretch forth thine hand against the wrath of mine enemies, and thy right hand shall save me.

– Psalm 138:7

Congratulations!

You are the catalyst for something great.

And she spake out with a loud voice, and said, Blessed art thou among women, and blessed is the fruit of thy womb. And whence is this to me, that the mother of my Lord should come to me? For, lo, as soon as the voice of thy salutation sounded in mine ears, the babe leaped in my womb for joy.

-- Luke 1:42-44

DAY 247

Congratulations!

You are taking control of ever distraction.

And this I say for your own profit, not that I may put a leash on you, but for what is proper, and that you may serve the Lord without distraction.

-- 1 Corinthians 7:35, NKJV

Congratulations!

Your progress is unstoppable!

For the Lord your God is he that goeth with you, to fight for you against your enemies, to save you.

-- Deuteronomy 20:4

Congratulations!

You will no longer feel powerless.

For God hath not given us the spirit of fear; but of power, and of love, and of a sound mind.

-- 2 Timothy 1:7

Congratulations!

The wind of change is blowing your way.

The wind blows where it wishes, and you hear the sound of it, but cannot tell where it comes from and where it goes. So is everyone who is born of the Spirit.

– John 3:8, NKJV

Congratulations!

You can expect a great return.

Give, and it shall be given unto you; good measure, pressed down, and shaken together, and running over, shall men give into your bosom. For with the same measure that ye mete withal it shall be measured to you again.

– Luke 6:38

Congratulations!

You have been called out and set apart.

For I am persuaded, that neither death, nor life, nor angels, nor principalities, nor powers, nor things present, nor things to come, nor height, nor depth, nor any other creature, shall be able to separate us from the love of God, which is in Christ Jesus our Lord.

– Romans 8:38-39

Congratulations!

God knows you by name.

But now thus saith the LORD that created thee, O Jacob, and he that formed thee, O Israel, Fear not: for I have redeemed thee, I have called thee by thy name; thou art mine.

– Isaiah 43:1

DAY 254

Congratulations!

God will fight for you.

The L ORD shall fight for you, and ye shall hold your peace.

-- Exodus 14:14

Congratulations!

God thinks about you.

How precious also are thy thoughts unto me, O God! how great is the sum of them!

-- Psalm139:17

DAY 256

Congratulations!

God has plans for you.

For I know the thoughts that I think toward you, saith the LORD, thoughts of peace, and not of evil, to give you an expected end.

-- Jeremiah 29:11

Congratulations!

God is your refuge.

Trust in him at all times; ye people, pour out your heart before him: God is a refuge for us. Selah.

-- Psalm 62:8

Congratulations!

God is always with you.

Teaching them to observe all things whatsoever I have commanded you: and, lo, I am with you always, even unto the end of the world. Amen.

-- Matthew 28:20

Congratulations!

Your deliverance doesn't need people's approval.

And Hannah answered and said, No, my lord, I am a woman of a sorrowful spirit: I have drunk neither wine nor strong drink, but have poured out my soul before the LORD.

-- 1 Samuel 1:15

Congratulations!

Do everything in love.

Love is patient, love is kind. It does not envy, it does not boast, it is not proud. It does not dishonor others, it is not self-seeking, it is not easily angered, it keeps no record of wrongs.

-- 1 Corinthians 13:4-5, NIV

Congratulations!

You have no need to fear or be in dread of your enemies.

Be strong and of a good courage, fear not, nor be afraid of them: for the LORD thy God, He it is that doth go with thee; He will not fail thee, nor forsake thee.

-- Deuteronomy 31:6

Congratulations!

Your spirit is unbreakable!

This hope we have as an anchor of the soul, both sure and steadfast, and which enters the *PRESENCE* behind the veil.

-- Hebrews 6:19, NKJV

Congratulations!

Your capacity will be expanded.

The thief cometh not, but for to steal, and to kill, and to destroy: I am come that they might have life, and that they might have it more abundantly.

– John 10:10

Congratulations!

Your gift is waiting for you.

For the wages of sin is death; but the gift of God is eternal life through Jesus Christ our Lord.

– Romans 6:22-23

Congratulations!

The King of kings is equipping you for every good work.

For the perfecting of the saints, for the work of the ministry, for the edifying of the body of Christ:

-- Ephesians 4:12

DAY 266

Congratulations!

You can cut the cord.

The LORD is righteous: he hath cut
asunder the cords of the wicked.

– Psalm 129:4

Congratulations!

The blessings of God will overtake you until you will not be able to keep track of them.

And all these blessings shall come on thee, and overtake thee, if thou shalt hearken unto the voice of the LORD thy God.

-- Deuteronomy 28:2

273

Congratulations!

You can leap again.

And he leaping up stood, and walked,
and entered with them into the temple,
walking, and leaping, and praising God.

-- Acts 3:8

Congratulations!

You going through this transition is better than you being stuck in it.

And he said, Let me go, for the day breaketh. And he said, I will not let thee go, except thou bless me.

– Genesis 32:26

Congratulations!

Either way it goes it is still victory.

For the LORD your God is he that goeth with you, to fight for you against your enemies, to save you.

– Deuteronomy 20:4

Congratulations!

God is going to invade your grieving and turn it into joy.

Then shall the virgin rejoice in the dance, both young men and old together: for I will turn their mourning into joy, and will comfort them, and make them rejoice from their sorrow.

-- Jeremiah 31:13

Congratulations!

No temptation has overtaken you that is not common to man.

There hath no temptation taken you but such as is common to man: but God is faithful, who will not suffer you to be tempted above that ye are able; but will with the temptation also make a way to escape, that ye may be able to bear it.

-- 1 Corinthians 10:13

Congratulations!

You do not need to be afraid of anyone.

And the LORD said unto Joshua, Fear them not: for I have delivered them into thine hand; there shall not a man of them stand before thee.

-- Joshua 10:8

DAY 274

Congratulations!

You are an overcomer.

These things I have spoken unto you, that in me ye might have peace. In the world ye shall have tribulation: but be of good cheer; I have overcome the world.

– John 16:33

Congratulations!

You will establish a supernatural environment for miracles.

And these signs shall follow them that believe; in My name shall they cast out devils; they shall speak with new tongues;

-- Mark 16:17

Congratulations!

Your past has nothing new to say to you.

Brethren, I do not count myself to have apprehended; but one thing *I do,* forgetting those things which are behind and reaching forward to those things which are ahead, I press toward the goal for the prize of the upward call of God in Christ Jesus.

-- Philippians 3:12-14

Congratulations!

The Jesus in you can speak to any storm.

And he saith unto them, Why are ye fearful, O ye of little faith? Then he arose, and rebuked the winds and the sea; and there was a great calm.

-- Matthew 8:23-27

Congratulations!

We have the same power that allowed Jesus to get up from the grave, working in us.

And Jesus came and spake unto them, saying, All power is given unto me in heaven and in earth.

-- Matthew 28:18

Congratulations!

The same place where your character was tested will be the place of your elevation.

When I was a child, I spake as a child, I understood as a child, I thought as a child: but when I became a man, I put away childish things.

-- 1 Corinthians 13:11

Congratulations!

You will have faith that produces results.

Now faith is the substance of things hoped for, the evidence of things not seen.

-- Hebrews 11:1

Congratulations!

You will no longer live beneath your privilege.

Fear thou not; for I *am* with thee: be not dismayed; for I *am* thy God: I will strengthen thee; yea, I will help thee; yea, I will uphold thee with the right hand of my righteousness.

-- Isaiah 41:10

Congratulations!

Every delay is in your favor.

Being confident of this very thing, that he which hath begun a good work in you will perform *it* until the day of Jesus Christ.

-- Philippians 1:6

Congratulations!

Whatever has been over your head will break.

And it shall come to pass in that day, that his burden shall be taken away from off thy shoulder, and his yoke from off thy neck, and the yoke shall be destroyed because of the anointing.

-- Isaiah 10:27

Congratulations!

God will silence the voice of the accuser.

And I heard a loud voice saying in heaven, Now is come salvation, and strength, and the kingdom of our God, and the power of His Christ: for the accuser of our brethren is cast down, which accused them before our God day and night.

-- Revelation 12:10

Congratulations!

You are good enough.

For we are His workmanship, created in Christ Jesus unto good works, which God hath before ordained that we should walk in them.

-- Ephesians 2:10

Congratulations!

You are worthy of double honor.

Let the elders that rule well be counted worthy of double honor, especially they who labor in the word and doctrine.

-- 1 Timothy 5:17

Congratulations!

Get ready to live in total abundance.

The thief cometh not, but for to steal, and to kill, and to destroy: I am come that they might have life, and that they might have it more abundantly.

-- John 10:10

Congratulations!

Your "Yes, Lord" will activate your assignment.

Also I heard the voice of the Lord, saying, Whom shall I send, and who will go for us? Then said I, Here am I; send me.

-- Isaiah 6:8

Congratulations!

God is rewriting your story.

Therefore if any man be in Christ, he is a new creature: old things are passed away; behold, all things are become new.

-- 2 Corinthians 5:17

Congratulations!

The Holy Ghost is filling you until you overflow.

And it shall come to pass afterward, that I will pour out my spirit upon all flesh; and your sons and your daughters shall prophesy, your old men shall dream dreams, your young men shall see visions:

-- Joel 2:28

Congratulations!

Your time is now.

For He saith, I have heard thee in a time accepted, and in the day of salvation have I succored thee: behold, now is the accepted time; behold, now is the day of salvation.

-- 2 Corinthians 6:2

Congratulations!

Those who counted you out are coming back to apologize.

And the LORD turned the captivity of Job, when he prayed for his friends: also the LORD gave Job twice as much as he had before.

-- Job 42:10-11

Congratulations!

You have been equipped with greatness.

From whom the whole body fitly joined together and compacted by that which every joint supplieth, according to the effectual working in the measure of every part, maketh increase of the body unto the edifying of itself in love.

-Ephesians 4:12-16

Congratulations!

You have been given the increase.

The LORD shall increase you more and more, you and your children.

-- Psalm 115:14

Congratulations!

You have been chosen to win.

Then he asked Jesse, "Is this it? Are there no more sons?" "Well, yes, there's the runt. But he's out tending the sheep." Samuel ordered Jesse, "Go get him. We're not moving from this spot until he's here." Jesse sent for him. He was brought in, the very picture of health—bright-eyed, good-looking. GOD said, "Up on your feet! Anoint him! This is the one."

-- 1 Samuel 16:11-12, MSG

Congratulations!

The Holy Spirit is calling you back to focus on the promise.

And I will pray the Father, and He shall give you another Comforter, that He may abide with you forever;

-- John 14:16

Congratulations!

You will have unlocked doors to promotions.

For promotion cometh neither from the east, nor from the west, nor from the south. But God is the judge: he putteth down one, and setteth up another.

-- Psalm 75:6-7

Congratulations!

What once was a "no" will be turned into a "yes."

Isaiah, leaving, was not halfway across the courtyard when the word of GOD stopped him: "Go back and tell Hezekiah, prince of my people…I've listened to your prayer and I've observed your tears. I'm going to heal you…I've just added fifteen years to your life;"

-- 2 Kings 20:4-6a, MSG

Congratulations!

Your life is about to change significantly.

Therefore Sarah laughed within herself, saying, "After I have grown old, shall I have pleasure, my lord being old also?" And the LORD said to Abraham, "Why did Sarah laugh, saying, 'Shall I surely bear *a child,* since I am old?' Is anything too hard for the LORD?"

-- Genesis 18:12-14a, NKJV

Congratulations!

A table is going to show up in your situation.

Thou preparest a table before me in the presence of mine enemies: thou anointest my head with oil; my cup runneth over.

-- Psalm 23:5

Congratulations!

Your amazing life starts now.

He will wipe away every tear from their eyes, and there will be no more death or mourning or crying or pain, for the former things have passed away.

Rev 21:4, NIV

Congratulations!

Your season of blessing is at hand.

To everything there is a season, and a time to every purpose under the heaven.

-- Ecclesiastes 3:1

Congratulations!

Hope will not slip from you.

And hope maketh not ashamed; because the love of God is shed abroad in our hearts by the Holy Ghost which is given unto us.

-- Romans 5:5

Congratulations!

Your application has been approved by the most high GOD.

Those things, which ye have both learned, and received, and heard, and seen in me, do: and the God of peace shall be with you.

-- Philippians 4:19

Congratulations!

Children from your family will graduate from school.

Train up a child in the way he should go: and when he is old, he will not depart from it.

-- Proverbs 22:6

Congratulations!

People are no longer a problem; Jesus is the answer.

Jesus saith unto him, I am the way, the truth, and the life: no man cometh unto the Father, but by Me.

-- John 14:6

Congratulations!

It came to kill but it was unsuccessful.

No weapon that is formed against thee shall prosper; and every tongue that shall rise against thee in judgment thou shalt condemn. This is the heritage of the servants of the LORD, and their righteousness is of me, saith the LORD.

-- Isaiah 54:17

Congratulations!

Your children are returning from the enemies' land.

Behold, I will gather them out of all countries, whither I have driven them in mine anger, and in my fury, and in great wrath; and I will bring them again unto this place, and I will cause them to dwell safely: And they shall be my people, and I will be their God.

-- Jeremiah 32:37-38

314

Congratulations!

You will experience a newness, a vigor, and new life.

Create in me a clean heart, O God; and renew a right spirit within me.

-- Psalm 51:10

Congratulations!

You will put a demand on God's power.

And when the woman saw that she was not hid, she came trembling, and falling down before him, she declared unto him before all the people for what cause she had touched him, and how she was healed immediately. And he said unto her, Daughter, be of good comfort: thy faith hath made thee whole; go in peace.

-- Luke 8:47-48

Congratulations!

God has not abandoned you.

Let your conversation be without covetousness; and be content with such things as ye have: for he hath said, I will never leave thee, nor forsake thee.

-- Hebrews 13:5

Congratulations!

Every battle is not meant to be fought alone.

And he said, Hearken ye, all Judah, and ye inhabitants of Jerusalem, and thou king Jehoshaphat, Thus saith the LORD unto you, Be not afraid nor dismayed by reason of this great multitude; for the battle is not yours, but God's.

-- 2 Chronicles 20:15

Congratulations!

You are going from anxiety to fearlessness.

Be careful for nothing; but in everything by prayer and supplication with thanksgiving let your requests be made known unto God. And the peace of God, which passeth all understanding, shall keep your hearts and minds through Christ Jesus.

-- Philippians 4:6-7

Congratulations!

There is a prophecy and a promise being fulfilled in your life.

He it is, who coming after me is preferred before me, whose shoe's latchet I am not worthy to unloose.

-- John 1:27

Congratulations!

God will not forget your work and labor of love.

For God is not unrighteous to forget your work and labor of love, which ye have shewed toward his name, in that ye have ministered to the saints, and do minister.

-- Hebrews 6:10

Congratulations!

You are now awakened into your sudden season of abundance.

Give, and it shall be given unto you; good measure, pressed down, and shaken together, and running over, shall men give into your bosom. For with the same measure that ye mete withal it shall be measured to you again.

-- Luke 6:38

Congratulations!

Fear will not decide your fate.

For God hath not given us the spirit of fear; but of power, and of love, and of a sound mind.

-- 2 Timothy 1:7

Congratulations!

Distractions will no longer look like opportunities.

There hath no temptation taken you but such as is common to man: but God is faithful, who will not suffer you to be tempted above that ye are able; but will with the temptation also make a way to escape, that ye may be able to bear it.

-- 1 Corinthians 10:13

Congratulations!

You can walk away from what is hurting you.

And Jesus answered and said unto him, What wilt thou that I should do unto thee? The blind man said unto him, Lord, that I might receive my sight. And Jesus said unto him, Go thy way; thy faith hath made thee whole. And immediately he received his sight...

-- Mark 10:51-52

Congratulations!

The controversy was necessary for your success.

By this I know that thou favourest me, because mine enemy doth not triumph over me.

-- Psalm 41:11

Congratulations!

The word of God is your life style.

Thou art my hiding place; thou shalt preserve me from trouble; thou shalt compass me about with songs of deliverance. Selah.

-- Psalm 32:7

Congratulations!

You have everything you need; the Great I am providing is already for you.

But my God shall supply all your need according to his riches in glory by Christ Jesus.

-- Philippians 4:19

328

Congratulations!

God is about to shut the mouth of the naysayer in high places of power.

But when they deliver you up, take no thought how or what ye shall speak: for it shall be given you in that same hour what ye shall speak. For it is not ye that speak, but the Spirit of your Father who speaks in you.

-- Matthew 10:18-20

Congratulations!

God is about to push you from the back of the line to the front of the line.

So the last shall be first, and the first last: for many be called, but few chosen.

-- Matthew 20:16

Congratulations!

You are about to see the results of answered prayers!

And Hannah prayed, and said, My heart rejoiceth in the LORD, mine horn is exalted in the LORD: my mouth is enlarged over mine enemies; because I rejoice in thy salvation.

-- 1 Samuel 2:1

Congratulations!

Great is the Lord's faithfulness to you.

It is of the LORD's mercies that we are not consumed, because his compassions fail not. They are new every morning: great is thy faithfulness.

-- Lamentations 3:22-23

Congratulations!

The steadfast love of the Lord never ceases.

Therefore, my beloved brethren, be ye steadfast, unmovable, always abounding in the work of the Lord, forasmuch as ye know that your labor is not in vain in the Lord.

-- 1 Corinthians 15:58

Congratulations!

God mercies never come to an end.

It is of the LORD's mercies that we are not consumed, because his compassions fail not. They are new every morning: great is thy faithfulness.

-- Lamentations 3:22-23

Congratulations!

You are birthing purposed things.

Forasmuch as ye are manifestly declared to be the epistle of Christ ministered by us, written not with ink, but with the Spirit of the living God; not in tables of stone, but in fleshy tables of the heart.

-- 2 Corinthians 3:3

Congratulations!

You have an unstoppable life.

Fight the good fight of faith, lay hold on eternal life, whereunto thou art also called, and hast professed a good profession before many witnesses.

-- 1 Timothy 6:12

Congratulations!

The Lord will open up to you His good treasury.

The LORD shall open unto thee his good treasure, the heaven to give the rain unto thy land in his season, and to bless all the work of thine hand: and thou shalt lend unto many nations, and thou shalt not borrow.

-- Deuteronomy 28:12

Congratulations!

God is re-weaponizing you and getting you ready for the fight.

I have fought a good fight, I have finished my course, I have kept the faith:

-- 2 Timothy 4:7

Congratulations!

God is opening your understanding of His word.

And he said unto them, These are the words which I spake unto you, while I was yet with you, that all things must be fulfilled, which were written in the law of Moses, and in the prophets, and in the psalms, concerning me. Then opened he their understanding, that they might understand the scriptures,

-- Luke 24:44-45

Congratulations!

The dots are going to connect for you.

Thou wilt keep him in perfect peace, whose mind is stayed on thee: because he trusteth in thee. Trust ye in the LORD forever: for in the LORD JEHOVAH is everlasting strength:

-- Isaiah 26:3-4

Congratulations!

Things in your life that did not come together will be accomplished by the Spirit of the Lord.

But the Comforter, which is the Holy Ghost, whom the Father will send in my name, he shall teach you all things, and bring all things to your remembrance, whatsoever I have said unto you.

-- John 14:26

Congratulations!

Everything you need is already in the earth.

For all the land which thou seest, to thee will I give it, and to thy seed forever.

-- Genesis 13:15

Congratulations!

A battle has ended and favor is flowing to you.

For whoso findeth me findeth life, and shall obtain favour of the LORD.

-- Proverbs 8:35

Congratulations!

The titles, grants, and loans are yours.

Bring ye all the tithes into the storehouse, that there may be meat in mine house, and prove me now herewith, saith the LORD of hosts, if I will not open you the windows of heaven, and pour you out a blessing, that there shall not be room enough to receive it.

-- Malachi 3:10

Congratulations!

God will get what's *for* you *to* you.

So that we may boldly say, The Lord is my helper, and I will not fear what man shall do unto me.

-- Hebrews 13:6

Congratulations!

The Lord your God is great and He is greatly to be praised.

Great is the LORD, and greatly to be praised; and His greatness is unsearchable.

-- Psalm 145:3

Congratulations!

As far as your eye can see, God has given you His favor.

And the LORD said unto Abram, after that Lot was separated from him, Lift up now thine eyes, and look from the place where thou art northward, and southward, and eastward, and westward: For all the land which thou seest, to thee will I give it, and to thy seed forever.

-- Genesis 13:14-15

347

Congratulations!

You have enough strength to let go.

Let thine eyes look right on, and let thine eyelids look straight before thee. Ponder the path of thy feet, and let all thy ways be established. Turn not to the right hand nor to the left: remove thy foot from evil.

-- Proverbs 4:25-27

Congratulations!

God knows the way He is taking me even when I do not understand.

But he knoweth the way that I take: when he hath tried me, I shall come forth as gold.

-- Job 23:10

Congratulations!

God is not trying to take the blessing from you, but trying to give the blessing to you.

Give, and it shall be given unto you; good measure, pressed down, and shaken together, and running over, shall men give into your bosom.

-- Luke 6:38a

Congratulations!

God wants to bless your hand, your basket and your storehouse.

The LORD shall command the blessing upon thee in thy storehouses, and in all that thou settest thine hand unto; and he shall bless thee in the land which the LORD thy God giveth thee.

-- Deuteronomy 28:8

Congratulations!

Get ready for a quick return on your investment.

Tomorrow about this time I will send thee a man out of the land of Benjamin, and thou shalt anoint him to be captain over my people Israel, that he may save my people out of the hand of the Philistines: for I have looked upon my people, because their cry is come unto me.

-- 1 Samuel 9:16

Congratulations!

God birthed you for a reason.

For I know the thoughts that I think toward you, saith the LORD, thoughts of peace, and not of evil, to give you an expected end.

-- Jeremiah 29:11

Congratulations!

You will have new friends.

A man that hath friends must shew himself friendly: and there is a friend that sticketh closer than a brother.

-- Proverbs 18:24

DAY 349

Congratulations!

You will have fresh opportunities.

Behold, I will do a new thing; now it shall spring forth; shall ye not know it? I will even make a way in the wilderness, and rivers in the desert.

-- Isaiah 43:19

Congratulations!

God wants to bless you to the point where it cannot even be quantified!

The liberal soul shall be made fat: and he that watereth shall be watered also himself.

-- Proverbs 11:25

Congratulations!

You will overcome procrastination.

Know ye not that they which run in a race run all, but one receiveth the prize? So run, that ye may obtain.

-- 1 Corinthians 9:24

Congratulations!

You will have a new zip code.

Now the LORD had said unto Abram, Get thee out of thy country, and from thy kindred, and from thy father's house, unto a land that I will shew thee:

-- Genesis 12:1

Congratulations!

God is expanding your finances.

The blessing of the LORD, it maketh rich, and he addeth no sorrow with it.

-- Proverbs 10:22

Congratulations!

God is imparting new ideas to you and you will succeed.

Now unto him that is able to do exceeding abundantly above all that we ask or think, according to the power that worketh in us.

-- Ephesians 3:20

Congratulations!

God will give you the power and knowledge to get wealth.

But thou shalt remember the LORD thy God: for it is he that giveth thee power to get wealth, that he may establish his covenant which he sware unto thy fathers, as it is this day.

-- Deuteronomy 8:18

361

Congratulations!

God will help you turn nations back to Him.

All the ends of the world shall remember and turn unto the LORD: and all the kindreds of the nations shall worship before thee.

-- Psalm 22:27

Congratulations!

There are miracles with your name on them that are going to start moving in your direction.

The steps of a good man are ordered by the LORD: and he delighteth in his way.

-- Psalm 37:23

Congratulations!

God inhabits (lives in) your praise.

But thou art holy, O thou that inhabits the praises of Israel.

-- Psalms 22:3

Congratulations!

You have exactly what you need to start your miracle right now.

So that we may boldly say, The Lord is my helper, and I will not fear what man shall do unto me.

-- Hebrews 13:6

Congratulations!

You live by every word that comes from the mouth of God.

But he answered and said, It is written, Man shall not live by bread alone, but by every word that proceeds out of the mouth of God.

-- Matthew 4:4

Congratulations!

There are some blessings you don't see right now but you will see in the next days.

Arise, get thee to Zarephath, which belongeth to Zidon, and dwell there: behold, I have commanded a widow woman there to sustain thee.

-- 1 Kings 17:9

Congratulations!

God will give you the backing that you need with tranquility.

The LORD lift up his countenance upon thee, and give thee peace.

-- Numbers 6:26

Congratulations!

You will experience the benefits of an everlasting life.

For the wages of sin is death; but the gift of God is eternal life through Jesus Christ our Lord.

-- Romans 6:23

Congratulations!

Your confession will grant you salvation.

If you confess with your mouth that Jesus is Lord and believe in your heart that God raised him from the dead, you will be saved.

-- Romans 10:9, CSB

Congratulations!

You will have new mantles, anointings, and plans of action.

Instead of your shame you will have a double portion, And instead of humiliation they will shout for joy over their portion Therefore they will possess a double portion in their land, Everlasting joy will be theirs.

-- Isaiah 61:7, NASB

Congratulations!

You have been granted free access to eternal life.

For God so loved the world, that He gave His only Son, that whoever believes in Him should not perish but have eternal life.

-- John 3:16, ESV

Made in the USA
Columbia, SC
24 March 2020